YOUR LIFE MATTERS

BY

PASTOR MARVIN J. LOCKETT

YOUR LIFE MATTERS

Copyright © 2019 by Marvin Lockett
Printed in the United States of America

All rights reserved. No part of this publication may be reproduced, stored in a retrieval system, or transmitted, in any form or by any means, electronic, mechanical, photocopying, recording, or otherwise, without the written prior permission of the author.

Book design by Michael Abraham

Cover photo by Ben Jackson

ISBN 978-0-9967744-6-8

DEDICATION

This book is dedicated to my grandmother, Grace Johnson Lockett. My grandmother was a woman who dearly loved the Lord and lived life everyday with the hope of reaching her heavenly home. She made sure that I went to Sunday School, Vacation Bible Study, Choir Practice, and most definitely Sunday morning worship service. This instilled in me the tools that I would need when troubles and trials would come my way.

We didn't have much growing up but what we had was Faith. My grandmother taught me what Faith meant and if I would trust God enough, he would always be there for me and protect me from harm and danger.

During our difficult times, I could always hear her singing gospel music and\or hymns. I didn't understand at the time why she could be singing and appearing to be so joyful when were going through so much. However, as I got older I realized that it was her way of portraying what Faith really meant and that it provided her with encouragement and strength.

This book is dedicated to her memory and the life she portrayed before me. I look forward to seeing her again in our heavenly home. I love you, Grandma, and thank you for being the God fearing woman that you were and a true example of a Christian.

To God Be the Glory!

INTRODUCTION

As a Pastor, I realize that it's my responsibility to give as many positive tools to parishioners as possible as references for them along their life's journey. I find that tears of many are being shed because they just don't have the tools to adequately deal with life's issues.

The church seemingly has lost its voice within the community and people seem to be stuck in places they just can't seem to escape. I'm providing this book as a tool, a reference, to those who may need just a little push to keep moving forward. A few words of encouragement.

As I take this journey of life, I realize that there are so many people that have no hope, no sense of happiness or joy. It appears that people have become complacent in the stage of life they are in and aren't seeking or aren't interested in having a better life.

I have seen how young adults have been beaten down by negativity, unemployment, and financial despair so much that they can't seem to find their way.

So many people are dealing with depression, sickness, disease, and homelessness. Often people have no thought for those who are experiencing these situations and due to the lack of interest in their problems they become complacent or content in their situations and remain there.

Our lives are filled with so many difficulties, and often we are dealt a hand that takes us through many different emotions. We are hit with many problems that bring us down. We tend to hit bottom, go through feelings of hopelessness and despair, which in turn can to lead to depression.

Merriam-Webster defines hopelessness as having no expectation of good or success. If you feel hopeless you are unhappy and there seems to be no possibility of a better situation. Sometimes it feels like our circumstance or situation will last forever, like there is no end to the sadness or despair that we may feel. Sometimes it appears that we are constantly going through problems, which leads us to a state of depression.

Psalms 30:5 says "For his anger endureth but a moment: in his favor is life; weeping may endure for a night, but joy cometh in the morning."

The scripture says, "Weeping may endure for a night". What is the length of the night? Sometimes the night can last for days, weeks, months, or even years. The night represents the period of time in which you experience difficult situations. However, there is a promise with this scripture that after this period of time, we will again experience the joy that was lost.

I have had many times in my life that I have been down where it seems like no one cared for me. Like I was all alone, like my hardships had the best of me. Like my life didn't matter or have purpose. The more I tried to do things on my own, the more difficult life got. I had to learn that my life mattered and had purpose; everything that the enemy (satan) was having me feel inside was a lie.

We all have seen news on television where people, especially young people have committed suicide for many different reasons. We have friends who are dealing with depression and find it hard to smile or feel encouraged. This got me to thinking about stories within the bible that reflect how people were in situations were it appeared their lives didn't matter or had no purpose. Like they were outcast and had no sense of hope. This is the reason I decided to write this book with hopes that biblical scriptures will encourage the readers to hold on to God and his powerful hand.

We are assaulted everyday by tricks of the enemy. He assaults our thoughts, our emotions, and our sanity. Jesus says in John 10:10, "The thief cometh not, but for to steal, and to kill, and to destroy; I am come that they might have life and that they might have it more abundantly". However, what this scripture doesn't tell us is how, when, what, or where he will do these things. satan kills our hopes, steals our dreams, and attempts to destroy our lives.

With these constant attacks feelings of desperation and hopelessness appear. Again, like no one is concerned about our livelihood. Those who we think are closest to us, those who call themselves our friends are continuously walking around us seeing the lonely expression that is on our face. However, they never acknowledge us or never try to understand what we are going through. It's like they don't care, and often people make it feel like we don't exist. But you have to know and express to yourself that your life does matter and it does have purpose. It's sometimes hard to believe that we do have purpose due to all the bombardment of difficulties and unimaginable situations.

We encounter many issues and often end up moping

around, in tears, and depressed. Again, not understanding why we are feeling this way and begin to enquire of the Lord why we are like this. Why does it appear that no one cares about my issues? Have you ever thought that you are going through so much because God is molding you into someone great? Or have you ever thought that God is allowing hardships to be in your life to get the glory out of it? As you continue to read, I pray that you will find something that will encourage your heart and convince you that your life is important, and God cares for you. You have purpose. Not just physically but we have spiritual purpose. We matter to the body of Christ and knowing that God is breeding us into his likeness by allowing hardships to be a part of our daily living is his way of building character in us and divinely creating us into tools to be used by him.

We don't see what he is doing because we can't look beyond the pain, criticism, or suffering we are experiencing due to our situations. However, have you ever tried flipping the situation and gather the understanding that there is a reason behind all that you go through?

Growing up in rural McDowell County, West Virginia, there weren't many opportunities afforded to many except the thought of working in the local coal mines. Most didn't have much, except the love of family and the love for the Jesus Christ.

I grew up in a generation, when Michael Jordan was beginning his career, when Whitney Houston, Janet Jackson, Madonna, and Michael Jackson's careers were exploding. We looked up to them as did many. On the playground, we tried to imitate every move of Michael

Jordon. However, in doing so didn't make us him. We were still who we were, living in the same rural county, and living the best we knew how.

We admired the lives of these people but often forgot that just maybe one day we to may be someone that others would look up to. But, because we didn't have lots of money, or have as many material things as others, it was like our lives didn't matter and that we would live in this state of life forever.

I often wonder how different my life would have been if I would have had people in it that was encouraging me to be the best I could be. Telling me not to stop pressing my way and that I could be whatever I chose to be. Although there were some, it was just assumed that we would graduate high school and work in the mines or a fast food restaurant. There were examples of people who were making it to higher heights and deeper depths but after they had left the local community, who was left to remind us to keep striving?

It is my hope that after reading this book, you will be encouraged and know that there is more to you than meets the eye. You are important to others as well as the body of Christ. Your life truly matters. Read on and see how people who were considered to be outcast, diseased, or depressed found that their lives truly mattered and that they had purpose.

Most recently a movement that resonated within African American communities called "Black Lives Matter," swept through the country. It shed light on the life of young black men and women who were seemingly being targeted by police. This book is not racially biased, or based upon ethnicity. It's to let each of you know that all lives matter to the Lord and the body of Christ, and that we have been bought with a price by the shedding of the Blood of the Lord.

We are to encourage one another and lift each other up. We matter to each other.

This book is filled with examples of lives that didn't tend to matter to most. However, God found purpose in their lives and their life story definitely reflects that when others looked down upon them, it was just the beginning of God picking them up and changing their lives. When you're at the lowest point of your life, it's the right time and place for God to move and make your life more than you can ever imagine.

I pray that this book will give you the hope and strength to keep moving forward, believing that God hasn't brought you to where you are in life right now to leave you. Your future will be brighter than your past and God will enlarge and bring increase to every area of your life.

God bless you.

YOUR LIFE MATTERS

"Many of the afflictions are the righteous: but the Lord delivereth him out of them all"
Psalms 34:19

God cares for you and will be in place to deliver you from many difficult situations. Whether they be health conditions, relationships, or depression, God will deliver you.

We live in a time where it looks as though cancer, heart attacks, and disease are on the rise. We hear and see so much. How many times have you seen where someone has battled cancer for a lengthy period of time but during their sickness, they were a help to many others?

Often we question, why do we have to go through this, but maybe the answer should be why not? Have you ever thought that going through difficult health scares is to show others how strong God is in your life? To allow others to see your Faith in God? Sometimes just maybe God is allowing you to go through these situations to give you a testimony.

Maybe we can take a different look at our sickness and turn it around to say, though I may be ill, there is a purpose behind it. God will get the glory out of your life.

In the Gospel of Luke Chapter 4 verses 43-48 King James Version, we find a woman who had an issue of blood. She was bleeding profusely and uncontrollably. She could not find any help. She spent all she had searching for someone to help her.

> *Luke 4:43-48 "And a woman having an issue of blood twelve years, which had spent all her living upon physicians, neither could be healed of any, 44) Came behind him, and touched the border of his garment: and immediately her issue of blood was stanched. 45) And Jesus said, 'Who touched me?' When all denied, Peter and they that were with him said, Master, the multitude throng thee and press thee and sayest thou, who touched me? 46) And Jesus said Somebody hath touched me: for I perceive that virtue is gone out of me, 47) and when the woman saw that she was not hid, she came trembling and falling down before him, she declared unto him before all the people for what cause she had touched him, and how she was healed immediately 48) And he said unto her, Daughter be of good comfort: thy faith has made thee whole, go in peace.*

Examining the story of this woman, we notice that she is not mentioned by name. Her identity is unknown, however her story is most important. What we know about her is that she had a condition in which she could not stop bleeding, therefore the bible reflects this as an "issue of blood". There was no medical diagnosis or medical term given to her condition. No doctor could help her. Reading this scripture all we gather is that she could not be healed of her problem. It would be true to say that she felt hopeless or maybe even worthless. It appears that she had done nothing wrong but because of her condition she was a social outcast, alone. She dealt with this situation for twelve (12) years and could not find any relief.

I could hardly imagine how she really felt, not being able to hang out with anyone and not being able to have an intimate relationship with anyone. I'm sure she probably felt depressed, maybe even had the feeling of suicide. As a young girl she no doubt had dreams of doing great things with her life. I'm certain that she couldn't see her life as it was at this time.

This is where we should reflect on our own lives and see how maybe our dreams have not come true. Although not yet true, maybe just the means have been delayed not denied.

After graduating from Big Creek High School in War, WV, I had big dreams of becoming a U.S. Marshall or working as a federal agent. I wanted to be a law enforcement officer. However, things started coming towards me in which I started making the wrong decisions and ended up in a dark place. Things continued to come at me and I didn't know how to handle them or overcome them. Sadly, due to decisions I made, I found myself in the middle of a cocaine addiction. I was in a really bad place emotionally and depressed. Feeling somewhat hopeless because I couldn't shake this addiction it felt like this is where my life would end and no one even cared. Then one day I remembered a scripture found in

Philippian's 4:13, "I can do all things through Christ which strengtheneth me".

It gave me a sense of empowerment to win this fight.

I began to question the Lord as to why I had to go through so much. Something I believe this woman with the "issue of blood" had also done. She spent all that she had, went to physician after physician and still found no cure. She was determined to be a social outcast, unclean.

Let's look further into her story. A couple of things are happening here. First, fear has appeared to set up within her. She was fearful that she would never be healed of her problem. That she would be in this condition forever. Hopelessness set in, and she undoubtedly was ready to give up. She had seen everyone she knew to see, spent all her earnings, and still was found not to be any better. In fact, she was getting worse. But all of a sudden, she hears a commotion outside her window and realizes that the man in whom she has heard of named Jesus was just outside walking down her street.

She was about to give up, and now because she has these feelings of giving up, Jesus shows up. It's like the old gospel song, "He's an on time God". Yes, He is.

Now the second thing is beginning occur. Desperation. Her desperation to be delivered from her issue has turned into Faith. She now believes if she can get to Jesus she would be healed. She makes her way through the crowd, no doubt hearing people saying bad things about her, asking what she thinks she is doing. Where does this unclean woman think she is going? Although this may have been happening, she didn't allow this stop her.

Often when we lose hope, we become desperate and will do anything to get better. She reaches out by Faith and doesn't touch Him directly, however, grabs just enough of His robe and through her Faith she was healed. This story is not only a story of a miracle, but of one that reveals more to the fleshy eye. This woman's life had purpose, she mattered not only to the people of that time but to all that read of her. It shows us that when things look their worst God is ready to step in and perform his best. What we learn from this is, she had to go through this storm in her life to show us that things, no matter how bleak they appear, can change if we stretch out on Faith and believe that our circumstance does not and will not determine the outcome of our lives. That you will not always be this way. It may be a long time coming but you must know a change is coming for you. This woman had purpose. That purpose was to show us that if we hold out and believe that you matter, you will be delivered.

Don't allow your past to determine your future. Don't allow the negativity of family or friends discourage you from believing there is more to you than meets the eye.

It is very intriguing that this woman's condition couldn't be healed. Even though she spent all her money paying physicians and specialists, she never got any better. It was like God was allowing her to suffer so that we who read her story would have increased faith and belief that if God could heal her after all she had done for herself to no avail, that he could do it for any of us.

Jesus was on His way to visit the daughter of the ruler of a synagogue, named Jairus. She was sick unto death. Jairus was seeking the Lord to come lay hands on her so she could be healed.

Jesus was on his way with Jarius but in the Spirit realm, God was moving on behalf of the woman with the issue of blood, and although He was going to see about someone else, the need and the time for this woman to be delivered of her situation was now at hand.

Even though He was on his way to see about Jairus's

daughter, the need for this woman's deliverance was great. Her life was just as important as the daughter of this great ruler.

Her life's story is important to us because it shows us how we should never give up. No matter how long we have dealt with our issues, God is still able and ready to move on your behalf.

You may not have an issue of blood, but we all have some issues. Issues of depression, issues of addiction and alcoholism, health issues, financial issues, or maybe just issues of the heart. Whatever the issue may be, it was necessary to know this ladies' story and how important her life matters to us as it reveals her trust and faith in getting closer to Jesus Christ.

She had spent her life's savings, travelled near and far, and she remained the same. However, when she heard Jesus just outside her window, she decided to get to Him, but the press, the crowd was very large. She never gave up on getting close to Him; she kept going until her outstretched hand touched the hem of his robe.

She didn't let anything stop her. She had tried everything else. She didn't have any more money, there were no more doctors for her to see, and now her only hope was to get to Jesus. What was rising inside her was what we call faith.

She truly believed that if she could get close to the Lord, she would be healed. Immediately upon touching his robe, she was indeed healed. It's a lesson well taught that just getting close or closer to the Lord will do nothing but bring complete healing, deliverance, and provisions into your life.

Her life was important enough that her story had to be

told for many reasons. One was because God must get the glory out of all things, and the second, her commitment, dedication, and desire to get better was persistent. One word to describe this woman would be that she was a fighter. She never gave up, she kept fighting. Her life should be that example to us to never give up and to keep getting closer to God.

If we keep His Word on our minds and his love in our hearts, He will deliver you. Why? Because you matter to him, his people, and the kingdom of God.

John 8:36 (KJV) "If the Son therefore shall make you free, ye shall be free indeed".

"For We Wrestle Not Against Flesh and Blood, But Against principalities, Against Powers, Against The Rulers Of The Darkness Of This World, Against Spiritual Wickedness In High Places"
Ephesians 6:12

Again, I grew up in a small coal mining community of Bishop, McDowell County, West Virginia. It was a community full of life and people of all ages. We didn't have much but what we did have was love and Faith in the Lord Jesus Christ.

Financially we were sustained by the work of the local coal mines. Our fathers, grandfathers, and great-grandfathers all provided for us through the back-breaking pain of coal mining. So, as generations went by it was obviously assumed that we all would do nothing else but mine coal.

Growing up in such a community provided a great atmosphere for family, love, and friendship, however trying to figure out who or what I wanted to become proved to be very difficult. All we knew was that employment could be found in the mines. Although I had hopes and dreams, I couldn't see them for only seeing the things I didn't have.

Often struggling with life brings us to a state of mind that life may not bring much better to us. It was hard to stay positive or believe I could become more or achieve more due to all the doubt I heard.

The thief Christ was referring to was satan, hereto referred to as (the enemy). You will notice that I did not capitalize the name "satan" for we don't seek to magnify his name in any shape or form. The enemy comes to steal our hopes, destroy our dreams, and kill our futures.

Christ tells us of the enemy's attempt but does not exactly inform us as to how he will do this. I have found that the enemy uses many tools in his continuous assault on our minds and one such tool is jealousy.

Your life has purpose, its most important to others and to the body of Christ. Sometimes we don't really understand how important our lives mean to others especially those who appear to have no hope or future.

There is a wonderful story in the Old Testament in the book of Genesis. It's a story of a father's love for a son and the jealousy of his brothers. It's also a story of how when God finds favor in you, the enemy attempts to tear you down.

When we look at the story of Joseph, we find a story of a young man who God had began to reveal things through dreams. However, his brothers couldn't get excited or understand because of their jealousy. Due to the things that were happening to him as a young person, Joseph couldn't see what God was trying to do in his life and how great he was to become. Sometimes we can't see the hand of God moving due to the circumstances or situations we are enduring.

Genesis 37:3-4 New International Version (NIV), "3) Now

> *Israel loved Joseph more than any of his other sons, because he had been born to him in his old age; and he made an ornate robe for him. 4) When his brothers saw that their father loved him more than any of them, they hated him and could not speak a kind word to him".*

In reading these first scriptures we immediately find the enemy implanting the seed of jealousy in the minds of Joseph's brothers. This was the beginning of the spiritual assault on a young man that had purpose and favor with God. Why would his brothers be jealous of him? They were his flesh and blood. Love should have been what they felt instead of jealousy.

What is jealousy? Merriam-Webster defines jealousy as being hostile toward a rival; envious. Synonyms for the word are covetousness, resentment.

Sometimes we may not see what we are to become or that God is even working in us, but the enemy knows when God is raising you up for greater things and he doesn't want you to reach those goals in Christ. He knows that you are important to God and His people therefore He begins his assault.

Have you ever thought that all the problems you endure, all the heartaches you experience, or even all the struggles you have, are only building your character? That it's preparing you for a greater and stronger you?

This is what young Joseph couldn't see. Often the doubt we verbally hear comes from those we are closest to. Our friends and family.

Joseph now was born to his father in his golden years. Due to this, his father loved him more. More so that he made him a coat of many beautiful colors. But now the enemy was understanding that there was something special about him and couldn't afford to allow him to reach his full potential, therefore causing a rift between those who meant the world to him, his family.

You must be able to look at things with your spiritual eyes and not only your fleshy ones. You must understand that troubles come to make you a stronger and more capable person.

As young people or young adults, we have dreams of achieving greatness. However, sometimes we fail to reach or accomplish those dreams. Does not accomplishing our goals make us any less important? Does it say that our lives don't matter?

Sometimes we fail to reach our dreams because we share our thoughts, our dreams, and our futures with others, who don't want to see you advance or live a life of purpose. Have you ever discussed something with someone, and all they could do was feed you with negativity so much that it deterred you from attempting to follow your dreams? Everyone that says they are on your side often is not.

Genesis 37: 5-11 says "5) Joseph had a dream, and when he told it to his brothers, they hated him all the more. 6) He said to them, Listen, to this dream I had, 7) We were binding sheaves of grains out in the field when suddenly my sheaf rose and stood upright, while your sheaves gathered around mine and bowed down to it, 8) His brothers said to him, "Do you intend to reign over us? Will you actually rule us?" And they hated him all the more because of his dream and what he had said. 9) Then he had another dream, and he told it to his brothers, "Listen, he said, I had another dream, and this time the sun and moon and eleven stars were bowing down to me, 10) When he told his father as well as his brothers, his father rebuked him and said, "what is this dream you had? Will your mother and I and your brothers actually come and bow down to the ground before you?" 11) His brothers were jealous of him, but his father kept the matter in mind."

Right off we see a few things happening. First God was revealing the future to Joseph but as a young person he couldn't see how God was preparing him and what would occur in his life. Second, we see how when we tell others about our hopes and dreams, even those who are the closest to us will not always support or be on board with what we are seeking to accomplish and therefore will seek to keep us right where we are in our present state of life.

Upon examining these scriptures, we see that God was revealing how great He would become. He was showing him that he had work to do and that he would be in position to lead and oversee. He was going to be in charge, having people under him.

Maybe young Joseph couldn't envision this because he was just a young shepherd, who was being disrespected by his family. God was starting to work on his life and his family could not understand. The spiritual attack on his life was beginning and his dreams were the target.

When the enemy is trying to harm you and keep your life stagnant, he doesn't just attack your life, he attacks the things that keep you hopeful and moving forward, which are your dreams.

God shows us things that are hard for others to

understand or comprehend. However, the one thing that should come to mind is that if God is revealing great things to you in dreams, you can guarantee that you have become important to Him and that your life matters.

Joseph did something that we do today and that is share our experiences, our dreams with people who should have understanding or be excited for us. However, when some people listen to what you say, they become jealous and attempt to discourage you by telling you what you can't do or explaining what won't happen in your life all because it hasn't happened in theirs.

Life is not perfect, but we do serve a perfect God. We must always be prayerful and be as tentative to the things that God is allowing to come our way. The trying times have purpose, sickness has purpose, trial & tribulations have purpose, you have purpose. Your life does matter.

Job 23:10 (NIV) states, "But he knows the way that I take; when he has tested me, I will come forth as gold".

Job states that wherever he went he felt as though God was there. He could not see what was going on but in verse 10 he writes that he knew that God knew where he was and the places he had been. Although he was being tried in the circumstances of life, he would eventually come out pure as gold. So, will you!!!! You must believe that you and your life matters.

To further discuss the jealous nature of people, the story of Joseph takes on a more dramatic course. Joseph's father sent him to check on his brothers who were tending flock in Shechem. As he approached, his brothers saw him afar and said, "Here comes the dreamer, let's kill him."

Genesis 37: 19 & 20 (NIV), "Here comes the dreamer, they said to each other. 20) Come now, let's kill him and throw him into one of these cisterns and say that a ferocious animal devoured him, then we'll see what comes of his dreams."

Maybe this sounds familiar in your life. That when people remember what you told them, with regards to your life or your dreams, they in turn attempt to entrap you. Destroy or criticize your thoughts of becoming more. I want you to know that the more the enemy attacks your life and\ or your dreams, the more God has for you. I get excited about this because the more he attacks the more powerful I become. When the enemy is attacking your hope, your thoughts or visions, this reveals that he knows that God has found favor with you and is establishing and preparing you for greater things. Praise God.

I have found that when God is about to open doors for you, when God is about to deliver you, the enemy will try his best to knock you down and hold you hostage. The good thing in being in Christ is that whatever the enemy does to deter you or whatever evil he brings your way, Jesus is more than able to turn it around for your good.

It's hard to see that sometimes because before that one thing gets turned around, something else happens. This is where you must stretch out on your faith and believe that no matter what you see or how bad you may feel, it's going to get better. As the song reflects, "Trouble Don't Last Always." It's a building block of your faith. Why do you suffer? Maybe it's for God to use you; you must be strong enough to handle the things he has in store for you. To be able to lead or witness to someone we must first be the example. To become greater, sometimes we must endure the hardships of life which build character.

Proverbs 3: 5 & 6 King James Version (KJV) says, "Trust in the Lord with all thine heart; and lean not unto thine own understanding. 6) In all thy ways acknowledge him, and he shall direct thy paths."

We may not be able to see why we are going through these things, but trust the Lord, acknowledge his greatness and he will reveal his plan for you. There is a spiritual plan for your life and following the spiritual plan leads to physical greatness.

Jeremiah 29:11 (NIV) says, "For I know the plans I have for you, declares the Lord, plans to prosper you and not to harm you, plans to give you hope and a future." We must keep the Faith and trust the work God is doing in our lives. Your life matters and this scripture reflects just that, and you must believe without a doubt that your suffering is not in vain, its just to let others know that God is molding you into a great warrior for Christ.

Jealousy, as we have read, is a treacherous tool and can't be allowed to ruin your future. God has so much more for you, and the enemy uses jealousy to keep you from moving forward. We are often unaware or maybe even a little naïve and think that everyone is on our side, when in fact this is not the case. There is an old saying, "misery loves company." This is often true, and others can't handle it when God is blessing you.

Jealousy is a tool of the enemy used more commonly by those we consider family or friends. You must stand firm and believe that no matter how difficult the matter, God will deliver you.

Growing up in such a small community provided a great atmosphere for family love and friendship, however trying to figure out who or what I wanted to become would prove to be very difficult. All we knew as kids was that employment could be found in the local coal mines. Although I had hopes and dreams, I couldn't see them for only seeing the things I didn't have. Often struggling with life brings us to a state of mind that life may not bring much better to us. It was hard staying positive or believing in becoming or achieving more, due to the doubt we were often fed.

> *In John 10:10, Jesus says, "The Thief cometh not, but for to steal, and to kill and to destroy. I am come that they might have life, and that they might have it more abundantly".*

The thief Christ was talking about is satan, hereto referred to as (the enemy). He comes to steal our hope, destroy our dreams, and kill our future.

Christ tells us of the enemies' attempted assault on us. However, He doesn't specifically inform us as to how they will do it. I have found that the enemy uses many tools in his continuous assault on our minds and again jealousy ranks high on the list.

Your life has purpose, it's most important to others and to the body of Christ. Sometimes we don't really understand how important our lives are to others, especially those who appear to have no hope or future.

We all have family members who have had opportunities to advance or do great things and just because they couldn't make it, they will be the very ones that will speak doubt into your life and encourage you to strive for less instead of more. They have become complacent with their lives and want you to be also with yours. However, when God opens doors for us, we must step through them. Why? Because the opportunity that God is creating is because you have purpose.

Sibling love is supposed to be perfect love. It supposed to be such that you would have one another's back, no matter what. However, this was not the case, and they couldn't support him, but instead wanted to harm him.

You must be able to look at things with spiritual eyes, not just with your fleshy ones. You must understand that trouble comes to make us stronger and more capable. Tests give you a testimony; trials if you endure make you better.

So as young people or young adults, we have dreams of achieving greatness. However, sometimes we fail to reach those or accomplish these things because we have shared them or our thoughts with people who don't want to see you advance or live a life with purpose.

Genesis 37:5-11 (NIV) 5) Joseph had a dream and when he told it to his brothers, they hated him all the more, 6)He said to them, Listen to this dream I had, 7) We were binding sheaves of grain out in the field when suddenly my sheaf rose and stood upright, while your sheaves gathered around mine and bowed down to it", 8) His brothers said to him, 'Do you intend to reign over us? Will you actually rule us?' And they hated him all the more because of his dream and what he had said. 9) Then he had another dream, and he told it to his brothers, 'Listen,' he said, 'I had another dream and this time the sun and moon and eleven stars were bowing down to me,'

10) When he told his father as well as his brothers, his father rebuked him and said, 'What is this dream you had? Will your mother and I and your brothers actually come and bow down to the ground before you?' 11) His brothers were jealous of him, but his father kept the matter in mind".

Sometimes God shows us things that are hard for others to understand or believe. However, the one thing that should come to mind is that if God is revealing great things to you in dreams, you can be guaranteed that you have become important to Him and that your life truly does matter and you have purpose.

Job 23:8-10 states, wherever Job went he felt as if God was not there, he could not see what was going on. However, he writes in verse 10 that he knew God knows where he was and places he had been. Although he was being tried in the circumstances of his life, he would eventually come out pure as Gold. SO, WILL YOU!!! You must believe that your life matters.

Job 23:8-10 (NIV) 8) "But if I go to the east, he is not there; if I go to the west, I do not find him. 9) When he is at work in the north, I do not see him; when he turns to the south, I catch no glimpse of him. 10) But he knows the way that I take; when he has tested me, I will come forth as gold".

To further discuss the jealous nature of people, the story of Joseph takes on a more dramatic course. Joseph's father sent him to check on his brothers, who were tending flock in Shechem. As he approached his brothers, they saw him afar off in the distance and said to one another, here comes the dreamer. Let's kill him.

Genesis 37: 19 & 20 (NIV) 19) "Here comes that dreamer", they said to each other. 20) Come now and let's kill him and throw him into one of these cisterns and say that a ferocious animal devoured him. Then, we'll see what comes of his dreams".

Maybe this sounds familiar in your life. That when people remember what you told them with regards to your life or your dreams, they, in turn, attempt to entrap you. Destroy or criticize your thoughts of becoming more. But I come to find that the more the enemy attacks you the more God has for you.

"We Are Troubled On Every Side, Yet Not distressed; We Are Perplexed, But Not In Despair; Persecuted, But Not Forsaken; Cast Down, But Not Destroyed"
2 Corinthians 4: 8-9

The issues of life are many and handling them in a successful way often proves to be difficult, but an old gospel song where the lyrics are, "I will Trust in the Lord, I will Trust in the Lord, I will Trust in the Lord until I die", and the last verse says, "I'm going to watch, fight, and pray, I'm going to watch, fight, and pray, I'm going to watch, fight, pray until I die."

This song provides encouragement and directs us in what to do when troubles come. One thing I am certain of is that trouble doesn't always last. However, sometimes it feels as if we will be in our present situation forever, and there is not way out. There is a great hope that must live inside you and that hope is Jesus Christ. You may be down but never without hope.

Looking again at the life of Joseph,

Genesis 37: 23-28 says, 23) And it came to pass, when Joseph was come unto his brethren that they stripped Joseph out of his coat, his coat of many colours that was upon him; 24) And they took him and cast him into a pit: and the pit was empty, there was no water in it. 25) And they sat down to eat bread: and they lifted up their eyes and looked and behold, a company of Ishmaelites came from Gilead with their camels bearing spicery and balm and myrrh, going to carry it down to Egypt, 26) And Judah said to his brethren, What profit is it if we slay our brother, and conceal his blood? 27) Come, and let us sell him to the Ishmaelites and let not our hand be upon him; for he is our brother and our flesh. And his brethren were content. 28) Then there passed by Midianite merchantmen; and they drew and lifted up Joseph out of the pit, and sold Joseph to the Ishmaelites for twenty pieces of silver: and they brought Joseph into Egypt."

Now we remember that God had revealed significant things to Joseph in his dreams and upon reading we know that Joseph's life had purpose and because of this his brothers were jealous and decided to get rid of him.

Joseph was loved by his father and envied so much by his brothers, the enemy could not stand to see how God was preparing him for his future. Thus became the evil plan to tear him down and attack his life.

Have you ever noticed a time in your life when you had thoughts of doing big things, such as getting a degree? Or maybe it was a big move to another city? Or maybe changing jobs? And when you got close to finalizing your decision, doubt crept into your mind, problems began to arise, and it eventually kept you from doing those things?

That's how the enemy tries to keep you down. When things start to open for you and you begin the contemplate making a move to better yourself, the enemy will start a move of concern or worry to distract you.

Joseph was going to be mighty and the enemy wanted to get rid of him. He wanted to kill him but when God has a plan for you the enemy can't stop it. Only you can.

Our lives are a lot like Joseph's, though he wasn't killed, he was sold into slavery. Our friends, family, or even co-workers sometime will attempt to sabotage or sell us out to keep from reaching our full potential, getting that job promotion, or even having that potentially permanent relationship you have been praying for all because you have purpose. Don't ever think your life is less important or that you don't have purpose. You matter.

We have people in our lives that will sell us out just to keep us from moving forward. Remember God's hand is upon us even when we don't feel as though He is near. When the enemy has set a trap and thinks he has you down, God always has a way of escape for you.

The Apostle Paul wrote in his letter to the Romans in, *Romans 8: 28 "And we know that all things work together for good to them that love God, to them who are the called according to his purpose".*

Your life is important, and it matters not only to others, but most importantly to God. We get down and go through so many battles, but you must know that when you are down, you must get up. Reach out by faith and grab hold to God's hand. It's always there waiting for you to hold onto.

In this journey of life, we often we see people who have been through so much. It's like when we look at them, we say to ourselves, how much more can they take. Life has worn them down and to continue to get up from a continual beat down becomes hard to do.

It's like a boxer in a twelve (12) round match. If he continues to get knocked down round after round it becomes much harder to get up and have the drive inside to continue the fight.

What keeps a person moving forward amid despair? What happens to a person's hope when he or she can see nothing but always being knocked down? We can't really see how strong we are because of the continuous battles we fight. We can't see ourselves getting up because we always seem down.

Often, we don't realize how important our getting up is to others. We don't understand what God is truly doing to do in our lives. All we see are the trials and tribulations that are before us. Giving up is the easiest thing to do. However, quitting or giving up gets us nowhere. It keeps you right where the enemy wants you, in a hopeless state of mind.

The most important thing that Joseph shows us is that each time the enemy thought he had him down, God intervened. Why was it important for God to intervene on behalf of Joseph? My answer would be that God knew that Joseph's life would show readers like us that no matter how dim the situation our lives have purpose.

"Remember Me, O Lord, With The Favor That Thou bearest Unto Thy People: O Visit Me With Thy Salvation"
Psalms 106:4

There are times when it feels like there is no end to the onslaught of attacks from the enemy. We don't know exactly what or how to think. How to function or what to do. It's difficult to see that God has you right where he wants you. It appears that we're all alone and God's grace and mercy can't be felt.

Sometimes we must look at things differently and understand that if we are going through continuous hardships, it must mean that God is doing something special in your life. He's building you up. He is there and his favor is with you.

Deuteronomy 31:6 (NIV), "Be strong and courageous. Do not be afraid or terrified because of them, for the Lord your God goes with you: he will never leave you nor forsake you".

This scripture is a direction to us to be strong and brave, not afraid of the situations or circumstances before you because the Lord God is with us.

As we find ourselves amid hardships, we must believe that God's favor will shine on us and deliver us from the problems.

As we have read a little about how people were jealous of

Joseph, we are going to see how the favor of God proved to be his deliverer as it will be for you.

Genesis 39:1-6 (KJV) says, "1)And Joseph was brought down to Egypt: and Potiphar, an officer of Pharoah, captain of the guard, an Egyptian, bought him of the hands of the Ishmaelites, which had brought him down thither, 2) And the Lord was with Joseph, and he was in the house of his master, the Egyptian. 3) And his master saw that the Lord was with him, and that the Lord made all that he did to prosper in his hand. 4) And Joseph found grace in his sight, and he served him: and he made him overseer over his house, and all that he had, he put into his hand. 5) And it came to pass from the time that he made him overseer in his house, and overall that he had, that the Lord blessed the Egyptians house for Josephs sake; and the blessing of the Lord was upon all that he had in the house, and in the field. 6) And he left all that he had in Joseph's hand; and he knew not ought he had, save the bread which he did eat. And Joseph was a goodly person and well favored".

Getting down on ourselves, feeling hopeless, and lacking the faith to believe in ourselves is truly a trick of the enemy. It makes it hard for us to see what others may indeed see in us. It makes it difficult for us to understand that our lives matter.

You may be saying to yourself, why I keep repeating this phrase over and over. The reason is that the more you tell yourself that your life has purpose and that it matters, the more you will start believing in yourself. You will begin to start saying it within yourself often, which in turn will make you stronger, more confident, and encouraged.

Joseph may not have seen that God was with him and that Heaven had found favor in him, but as we continue to read this story, we should be able to get excited about our own story.

Believing that if God did all of that to show us that Joseph had purpose, and then he truly can do it for us. There is nothing that God can't do for you. He can't fail you. He won't fail you.

Now Joseph had been sold off into slavery by those he thought loved him. They thought they were sending him off into a life of pain and suffering but watch what happens.

As the Ishmeelites came into Egypt, Potiphar, the Captain of the Guard, purchased him. The scripture tells us that the Lord was with Joseph and was a prosperous man.

Potiphar undoubtedly saw something in Joseph. There had to be something different about him. Maybe he didn't look filthy or lowly like a slave. Maybe his appearance was that of a person who stood out in a crowd. Maybe there is something unique in you that you can't see or believe, but God does and allows others to see it and use it to his glory.

No matter what Potiphar saw, it was God's plan in motion. It was God's plan for these things to happen in this sequence of Joseph's life. Have you ever wondered that the order of events happening in your life is God's plan for you in Order to get you where he needs you to be?

Joseph, a slave, who had been cast into a pit, left to die, then sold into slavery is now being described as a prosperous man. Living in the house of his master.

Our spiritual eyesight is often obstructed by the fleshy

feelings of depression and oppression. We are blinded and just can't see what God is doing. Therefore, we must depend on what someone else sees in you.

His master realized that there was truly something special about this young man and that he needed to keep him close. After realizing that God was with Joseph and that he made all that he did prosper in his hand, his master made him overseer over his house and all that he had.

Joseph had come from the pit to the palace. When it appears that all is lost. When it looks as though you can't make it out of your circumstance, that's when God wants to show you that he's got your back and he needs you to help someone else.

His brothers threw him to the side. They discarded him like trash and now Joseph found himself living a life of leadership, riches, and greatness. When no one else cared what would happen to him, he now was overseeing all that the Captain of the Guard owned.

Often, we have friends, family, co-workers, who treat us like dirt or like we don't even matter. They could care less if you prospered or fell flat on your face.

However, in this wonderful story of Joseph, I didn't notice one time where Joseph was moping, crying, or making any excuses about the things that was happening in his life. He just held on realizing that this battle belonged to God and he had to trust the process.

2 Chronicles 20:15 (KJV) reads, "And he said, Hearken ye, all Judah, and ye inhabitants of Jerusalem, and thou King Jehoshaphat, Thus saith the Lord unto you, Be not afraid or dismayed by reason of this great multitude: for the battle is not yours, but God's."

Our flesh wants to fall to pieces. It wants to rage and start to fight back. It wants to cry and whine, but our faith must remain in Christ and not interfere with his process. God is in control of your life. You must believe and trust his process. If God can do this for Joseph, how much more can he do for you?

We sometimes mess up our own lives by interfering with how God is directing it. We give blame to the enemy and everyone, when we ourselves are the cause of our disheartening situations. The above referenced scripture says for us to not be afraid or dismayed by what we see or by what we feel. Our battles belong to God.

You may have been discouraged, down, or broken, and left to cry in your mess. Does this mean that your life means any less? No, it's just the start of a new you. You just have to hold on and trust the Lord and his process for your life. If you just trust him, grace and mercy will deliver you.

Now after God has brought you through your difficult moments, restored your confidence, restored your smile, and has blessed you abundantly, you need to know that the enemy is not happy and is contemplating his next attack on your life. Why? Because he wants the thoughts of you living a purpose filled life to be short-lived and die.

When the enemy sees how blessed you are and how much you mean to Christ and his people, he will seek to destroy you in many ways.

Jesus says in,

John 10:10 (KJV), "The thief cometh not but for the steal, and to kill, and to destroy: I am come that they might have life and that they might have it more abundantly".

Jesus doesn't state how the enemy would come, that why we must be vigilant and in constant connection with the Lord.

Joseph had been blessed beyond measure and had received not just the favor of God but also that of his owner. He had been blessed so much that his owner became more prosperous because of him. But now the enemy was not happy and was seeking a way to destroy Joseph and the attack came against him in the form of a lie.

Genesis 39:7-16 (KJV) reads "7) And it came to pass after these things, that his master's wife cast her eyes upon Joseph, and she said, Lie with me. 8) But he refused, and said unto his master's wife, Behold, my master wotteth not what is with me in the house, and he hat committed all that he hath to my hand; 9) There is none greater in this house than I; neither hath he kept back anything from me but thee, because thou art his wife: how then can I do this great wickedness, and sin against God? 10) And it came to pass, as she spake to Joseph day by day, that he hearkened not unto her to lie by her, or to be with her. 11) And it came to pass about this time, that Joseph went into the house to do his business: and there was none of the men of the house there within. 12) And she caught him by his garment, saying, Lie with me: and he left his garment in her hand, and fled, and got him out. 13) And it came to pass when she saw that he had left his garment in her hand, and was fled forth, 14) That she called unto the men of her house, and spake unto them, saying, See, he hath brought in an Hebrew unto us to mock us: he came in unto me to lie with me, and I cried with a loud voice: 15) And it came to pass

> *when he heard that I lifted up my voice and cried, that he left his garment with me, and fled and got him out. 16) And she laid up his garment by her until his Lord came home".*

Now we usually automatically believe the voice of family instead of others. We pronounce judgment before we seek the truth. However, as her spouse, Joseph was inclined to believe her if he wanted to keep a happy home.

The enemy has initiated the lie with all intent and purpose of destroying Joseph's life. But again, his life mattered and had purpose. All lies are born in hell and are the product of satan. The one thing that satan cannot do is tell the truth.

> *John 8:44 God's Word Translation (GW) says, "You come from your father, the devil, and you desire to do what your father wants you to do. The devil was a murderer from the beginning. He has never been truthful. He doesn't know what the truth is. Whenever he tells a lie, he's doing what comes naturally to him. He's a liar and the father of lies".*

This new attack on Joseph came because the enemy was upset that God kept turning things around for him. Could be that Potiphar's wife was jealous due to the attention and liberty he had given Joseph, in that he oversaw everything they owned.

Now the lie was out in the air and believed by Potiphar. It infuriated him so much that he threw Joseph into prison. However, when God is with you, there's nothing that can keep you down. The enemy may cause temporary harm, but God's favor will always provide a way of escape for you.

Joseph now found himself incarcerated in a place where

the King's prisoners were bound. In reading that, it got me to thinking about how often we find ourselves incarcerated in our own depression, how we are sometimes incarcerated in hopelessness. We must believe that when we are spiritually incarcerated in these forms of battles, there is a moment that will come to set you free.

Joseph was incarcerated but scripture let's us know that the Lord was with him. Even incarcerated he had the favor of God upon him.

Genesis 39:21-23, "21) But the Lord was with Joseph, and showed him mercy and gave him favor in the sight of the keeper of the prison. 22) And the keeper of the prison committed to Josephs hand all the prisoners that were in the prison; and whatsoever they did there, he was the doer of it. 23) The keeper of the prison looked not to anything that was under his hand; because the Lord was with him, and that which he did, the Lord made it to prosper."

Lies can be hurtful and can cause a lot of pain, however God can and will turn those lies around for your good.

Nothing was working. Everything that the enemy threw against Joseph, God turned it around for his good and caused him to prosper. He had purpose and his life mattered.

Romans 8:28 (KJV), "And we know that all things work together for good to them that love God; to them who are the called according to his purpose"

When things look bleak and you seem depressed, you must believe and say within yourself that Christ is turning things around for me. If he caused things to turn around for Joseph, he can do the same for you. Why? Because your life matters.

"And let us not be weary in well doing; for in due season we shall reap, if we faint not.
Galatians 6:9

I love this scripture because it's a promise that we can stand firm on. However, it often proves difficult when one thing after another keeps happening. It gets tiresome fighting constant battles which never seem to subside. Continuously fighting through difficulties can make us weak -- physically and spiritually. But if we understand the reward awaiting us then we must have the hope of reaping a prosperous harvest.

As we examine the above scripture, it starts with a statement of encouragement to not allow yourself to fall weak in your struggle nor your purpose and or remain strong in the Lord and the power of his might.

Then it promises us that if we do so, God will allow us to experience our season of harvest, our season of breakthrough, even when all hope seems to have diminished. We must still be able to see God still moving in our midst.

Joseph is incarcerated and is now a supervisor over the entire jail. God's favor is still upon his life. But something is about to happen, which gives Joseph a false hope of being delivered.

Have you ever done something for someone and upon completion of your work, you ask them for a small favor?

Or maybe upon completion of your work or your help they offer to do something for you, as a blessing for your time or money. This is about to happen to Joseph which causes his flesh to believe that his new friends were about to help him get released from his incarceration.

I want to reiterate that your life matters. No matter what people fail to do for you, there is still something in you that the world must see. Someone is waiting to see what God is going to do in your life.

Pha'raoh was upset with two (2) of his officers: the Chief Butler and the Chief Baker. Insomuch as to put them in jail and Joseph was put over them.

Genesis 40:2-4, "2) And Pha'raoh was wroth against two of his officers, against the chief of the butlers, and against the chief of the bakers. 3) And he put them in ward in the house of the captain of the guard into the prison, the place where Joseph was bound. 4) And the captain of the guard charged Joseph with them, and he served them; and they continued a season in ward."

That last sentence resonates within me because many times people are put in your life, in your atmosphere, only for a season. Sometimes the season is short, but it could also prove to be lengthy, but there is purpose and lessons to be learned while the season last.

The baker and the butler both had dreams but had no idea of the interpretation of their dreams. Joseph looked in on them and saw they were sad and asked why.

They wanted to know the meaning of their dreams. Joseph decided to listen. The chief butler explained his dream in detail and Joseph afterwards interpreted the dream for him and he seemed very happy.

The interpretation was so good that it was well received by the butler. Joseph took this opportunity to ask the butler, that upon his release and when everything for him was once again going well with the King, to think about him, show kindness, and to mention his name to Pha'raoh, that he may be released.

After the butler was released and restored, he failed to remember Joseph and how he was blessed by his interpreting his dream and by the kindness that was shown towards him to the King. Now Joseph, having no doubt a mindset that he would soon be delivered from this incarceration found himself saddened and left in prison.

You could probably imagine how Joseph may have felt. He had helped someone with a problem and all he asked was to tell the King about him. Tell him his name and what he had done. All with hope that he would be released, and it never happened.

How tired and how mistreated he must have felt. Every time he turned around, something was happening to him, someone always seemed to be doing him wrong.

How his expectation of receiving something in return for his kindness was turned once again into heartache. However, he never gave up and never gave in.

Our reward for our good works toward men and women don't come from them but from the Lord. Our expectation should be that God will bless our good works towards one another.

In that his release from incarceration didn't happen in this time, it didn't mean that his blessing wasn't on the way.

In that his release was delayed it didn't mean that he was denied. We often look for our blessing from man, but we must first realize that the author of all blessings and all that is good, come from the Lord. However sometimes we must wait on Him, wait in faith, believing that there must be a reason you haven't been delivered, healed, or restored. There must be a purpose behind it all.

> "And the God of all grace, who called you to his eternal glory in Christ, after you have suffered a little while, will himself restore you and make you strong, firm, and steadfast."
> 1 Peter 5:10

When we are blessed, we are favored by God and being favored by God causes the enemy to be upset. Our adversary is unhappy and doesn't like when your Faith is strong, and things seem to be good in our lives. We must be watchful and prayed up ready for any attack he may bring upon us.

1 Peter 5:8 says, "Be sober, be vigilant; because your adversary the devil, as a roaring lion, walketh about, seeking whom he may devour:"

The one thing we must understand is that he can only do what God allows him to. So why would God allow trials and tribulations in our lives? Why would God allow us to experience negative situations and considerable hardships? German philosopher Friedrich Nietzsche said, "That which does not kill us, makes us stronger".

I believe this to be ever so true. Suffering, enduring troubles, and trials, build strength and character. What is important is what we do when we are experiencing these things.

Enduring hardships in Faith will bring you into a blessed

state of life that you couldn't have seen or realized until you went through the storms of life.

Job 1:1-3 (KJV) " 1) There was a man in the land of Uz, whose name was Job; and that man was perfect and upright, and one that feared God and eschewed evil. 2) And there were born unto him seven sons and three daughters. 3) His substance also was seven thousand sheep and three thousand camels, and five hundred yoke of oxen, and five hundred she asses and a very great household, so that this man was the greatest of all the men of the east."

This is a description of a person who had it all. He is described as a perfect and upright man, who had children, cattle, land, and money. Job was a great man.

But even when things are going just right, when things seem perfect, there is still more to you that hasn't come forth.

What more could Job ever want? What more did he need? He had all the material things he could want, however, there was more spiritually that God required of Job.

Even when it appears you have everything and have achieved the highest of heights and deepest depths. If you haven't given your life to Christ, you still haven't obtained the best that God has for you. You haven't reached your purpose.

Often it appears as though those who have everything are without troubles and\or problems and can buy themselves out of their situations. However, even the rich have problems, and yes, even the rich don't know or haven't understood their purpose.

For those of us who have children, we must find ourselves being the kind of parent or even grandparent that we find Job to be. Even though he had wealth he understood that it all came from God. He loved God and interceded in prayer on their behalf because he felt they may have sinned before God and he sought God's forgiveness on their behalf.

> *Job 1:4-5 "And his sons went and feasted in their houses, everyone his day, and sent and called for their three sisters to eat and drink with them. 5) And it was so, when the days of their feasting were gone about, that Job sent and sanctified them, and rose up early in the morning and offered burnt offerings according to the number of them all: for Job said, It may be that my sons have sinned, and cursed God in their hearts. Thus did Job continually."*

Job was truly a righteous man who not only loved God but loved his family. Job understood that his children were important to him and that it was his responsibility to keep them before the Lord.

But our adversary never quits and is always seeking to destroy those who God has predestined for greatness. He attempts to prevent us from not only understanding our purpose but to terminate the advancing of careers, hopes, or dreams.

Unbeknownst to Job, he would soon find himself in the middle of a very difficult experience. You could say he was in a war of good versus evil. You could even say it was a situation between who God knew Job to be or who our adversary wanted Job to become.

However you look at it, it was to be a life-altering

experience. A life-changing time that would wreak havoc in his life.

How do we react when life presents intense struggles to you or in your family's lives? The reaction to our problems either bring you out of them or extend them.

Our spiritual enemy is consistently looking to deter you from understanding God's purpose in you.

I need you to say to yourself at this moment, "I believe that my life has been bought with a price, the Blood of Jesus Christ and therefore my life rest in His hands. I can be whatever I want to be, I can go places I've never been before, and I can achieve things I seek. I belong to the Lord."

Repeat that to yourself everyday and watch God deliver greatness into your life.

Now we must understand that satan wishes to cause trouble and in the next text we find God having a conversation with him.

Job 1:7 (KJV), "And the Lord said unto satan, Whence comest thou? Then, satan answered the Lord and said, from going to and fro in the earth, and from walking up and down in it".

Then the unimaginable happens. God ask satan a question. Have you tried my servant Job? Oh my goodness!!!! Now we begin to question God as to why he would intentionally direct satan's attention to Job.

Why would God direct his attention to a man that is described as perfect and upright? One who strived for perfection in Godly living?

An answer could be that, God knew Job, just as He

knows you. God sometimes allows things to happen in your life that don't appear to be good, in fact they are often treacherous and life threatening. However, again I want to express that the way you react to life's issues will determine the length and\or severity your situations.

We should never be defined by our situations, but we should be defined by how we react to our situations.

Job didn't know or understand that the way he would handle his difficulties would be written for the purpose of encouraging the readers of today.

So, let's read and get an understanding of how God was going to allow satan to attack Job's life.

Job 1:8-12 "8) And the Lord said unto satan, Hast thou considered my servant Job, that there is none like him in the earth, a perfect and upright man, one that feareth God and escheweth evil? 9) Then satan answered the Lord, and said, Doth not Job fear God for nought? 10) Hast not thou made and hedge about him, and about his house, and about all that he hath on every side? Thou has blessed the work of his hands and his substance is increased in the Lord. 11) But put forth thine hand now, and touch all that he hath, and he will curse thee to thy face, 12) And the Lord said unto satan, Behold all that he hath is in thy power, only upon himself put not forth thine hand. So satan went forth from the presence of the Lord."

So, Job has no idea that he was the subject of a conversation between God and satan. He had no idea what was about to occur in his life, but God knew his heart and knew how much Job loved him and that he trusted in him.

So, as we read the above scripture, we must examine

ourselves and question whether God looks upon us in the way he did Job. Can he believe in you, as he believed in Job?

In reading the above scripture I also discovered that our adversary doesn't want to mess with those who are living in a blessed state of life because he knows God's hand is upon them. He knows when God is moving in and around your life, therefore doesn't want any part of you.

However, in this state of life, a blessed state of life, we must submerge ourselves in God's glory and anointing.

So, we now know that Job, unknowingly, is about to endure suffering like he has never seen. But God allowing these things to occur in Job's life was to purify and strengthen his faith. He had purpose and his purpose was to be that Godly example for us. His life had purpose and it mattered.

Your life matters. You have purpose. You must consider the question; would the enemy keep harassing you if your life didn't have meaning? Would you constantly be going through trials and tribulations if your life didn't have meaning to someone?

Struggle brings you to the arms of the Lord and opens great opportunity for you to achieve greatness; however, we fail to look at the bigger picture when we are in the midst of our problems. Life's problems make you stronger and build character within you.

You may be going through a situation at this moment, but this is your opportunity to speak positive over your life and believe that God is about to bring great things your way. You are about to see an explosion of God's glory in your life. Things at this very moment are about to change, as you will see it happen for Job.

Take this moment, raise your hands and tell God "Thank you" for turning things around for you.

1 Thessalonians 5:16-18, "16) Rejoice evermore, 17) Pray without ceasing, 18) In everything give thanks: for this is the will of God in Christ Jesus concerning you."

Now on a certain day, all was well with Job and the day started like it had any other day. However, all was about to change. Danger, hardships, and tragedy were approaching, and Job had no indication that his life was about to be turned upside down. Therefore, we must always be in constant prayer and under the anointing.

Job 1: 13-19 (KJV), "13) And there was a day when his sons and daughters were eating and drinking wine in their eldest brother's house, 14) And there came a messenger unto Job and said, 'The oxen were plowing and the asses feeding beside them,' 15) And the Sabeans fell upon them, and took them away; yea, they have slain the servants with the edge of the sword, and I only am escaped alone to tell thee. 16) While he was yet speaking, there came also another and said, 'The fire of God is fallen from heaven and hath burned up the sheep, and the servants, and consumed them; and I only am escaped alone to tell thee.' 17) While he was yet speaking, there came also another and said, 'The Chaldeans made out three bands and fell upon the camels, and have carried them away, yea, and slain the servants with the edge of the sword; and I only am escaped alone to tell thee.' 18) While he was yet speaking, there came also another and said, 'Thy sons and thy daughters were eating and drinking wine in their eldest brother's house:' 19) And behold, there came a great wind from the wilderness and smote the four corners of the house and it fell upon the young men and they are dead, and I only am escaped to tell thee."

Wow, and you think you have had bad days! I believe I can say with certainty that not one of our worst days could come close to the tragic day that Job was having.

Not only did Job lose his wealth, livestock, and servants, but he also lost his children. It's hard for me to imagine how one could retain their sanity after losing everything and everyone most important to you, all in one day.

There must be a purpose and a reason as to why all of this was happening. But what could it be? Did it take all of this tragedy to prove to us that God's Grace and Mercy is greater than anything the enemy can do to us?

One would immediately have to believe that Job had purpose in his life for all of this to happen to him at one time. Often when trials or conflicts occur in our lives, we have time in between them to organize our thoughts or our feelings. However, Job didn't have the luxury to take a breath because while he was getting bad news from one, another was showing up to give more.

Sometimes our purpose or the reaching of our purpose causes us to endure some difficult and trying times in our lives, but in all things we must be mindful that God is right there and is waiting for you to call His name so that He can hold your hand and lead you through your difficult times. Why? Because you matter to Him and your life has purpose.

Job demonstrates to us a response to his circumstance that is hard for us to comprehend and certainly difficult to perform.

Such loss would drive the average person to the brink of death or to the point of just not wanting to live. It would most definitely bring us into a state of severe depression. However, due to Job's relationship with God, he was able to understand that no matter how hurt, depressed, or devastated he was, he still had to honor, worship, and praise God.

Easier said than done you say, right? To enable this form of response, we must truly have an intimate relationship with our Lord Jesus Christ. We must believe that God is always in control of all things. No matter how they come. Whether it is in good times or in tragedy, he is always in control.

> *Job 1:20-22 (KJV), 20) Then Job arose, and rent his mantle and shaved his head and fell down upon the ground and worshipped. 21) And said 'Naked came I out of my mother's womb and naked I shall return thither: the Lord gave and the Lord hath taken away: blessed be the name of the Lord.' 22) In all this, Job sinned not, nor charged God foolishly.*

We must not become so immersed in our problems that we begin to blame God foolishly for them.

Job's reaction to his substantial loss reveals to us that when we are one with Christ, we can handle anything that comes our way.

Job understood that all he had wasn't based on how smart he was, who he knew, or how popular he may have been, Job knew that all he had obtained had come from God.

His strength was in knowing that God was in control.

The Lord gave and the Lord has taken away, blessed be the name of the Lord. Your strength in difficult times comes when you know that God is directing the traffic of your life.

What satan was counting on was for Job to give up on God. He was certain that if he tore Job's life apart that he would give up his love for God.

I'm reminded of a scripture written by the Apostle Paul in his letter to the Romans,

Chapter 8:35-39. "35) Who shall separate us from the love of Christ? Shall tribulation, or distress, or persecution, or famine, or nakedness, or peril or sword? 36) As it is written, For thy sake we are killed all the day long; we are accounted as sheep for the slaughter. 37) Nay, in all these things we are more than conquerors through him that loved us. 38) For I am persuaded, that neither death, nor life, nor angels, nor principalities, nor powers, nor things present, nor things to come, 39) Nor height, nor depth, nor any other creature, shall be able to separate us from the love of God, which is in Christ Jesus our Lord".

Job had purpose. He held firm to his trust in God. He was determined that no matter the situation he would never turn away from God.

Just as the above scripture states, although we're going to have our problems, we can overcome them, but the enemy never gives up. Now as we read further, another conversation is being held between God and satan about Job.

Job 2:1-6 (KJV) "1) Again there was a day when the sons of God came to present themselves before the Lord, and satan

came also among them to present himself before the Lord. 2) And the Lord said unto satan, from whence comest thou? And satan answered the Lord, and said from going to and fro in the earth, and from walking up and down in it. 3) And the Lord said unto satan, Has thou considered my servant Job, that there is none like him in the earth, a perfect and upright man, one that feareth God, and escheweth evil? And still he holdeth fast his integrity, although thou movedst me against him, to destroy him without cause. 4) And satan answered the Lord and said, skin for skin, yea all that a man hath will he give for his life. 5) But put forth thine hand now, and touch his bone and his flesh, and he will curse thee to thy face. 6) And the Lord said unto satan, Behold, he is in thine hand; but save his life."

As Job has gotten through the toughest time undoubtedly, he has every experienced, here comes another terrible situation.

Does this last scripture sound familiar? Here again God is allowing horrific circumstances to come against Job. satan is so sure that if he caused Job to experience bodily hurt or discomfort, he would forget about serving God.

The purpose of the writing of this Book of the Bible is to encourage the reader to understand that if Job can overcome his adverse situations, we can too.

Verses 5-6 reflect God's commitment to Job as well as to us. He speaks to satan and allows him to come against his health and everything he has but the saving grace in this is that God commands him not to take his life.

God was using Job's life as an example to us. Job's life was purposed for us to gain understanding, strength, and knowledge of overcoming the trials of life.

Have you ever had the thought come to your mind, "Why do these bad things keep happening to me?" Why God do you allow such hurtful things to occur in my life. Have you ever talked to God and say, "I'm just an ordinary person God, why does this keep happening?

It's OK to ask God why and I believe many of us have said these things to ourselves at some time in our quiet moments. But your life is important and has purpose. **God allows things to occur in ordinary people to reveal extraordinary things.**

Now God has told satan that he could do what he wanted but not to take his life. What confidence to know that satan may cause havoc yet God is still in control of it all.

satan, scripture tell us, leaves the presence of God and began to come against the health of Job. He couldn't destroy Job by killing his children and his cattle, so now he's trying to destroy his mind and mental state by causing health problems.

Job's previous loss should have been enough to break him. satan comes up against us to destroy our love and trust in God. By constantly going through hard times, it often causes our minds to become weary and what we know about Christ and his love for us becomes blurred. This causes a break in our bond with Jesus Christ, but he is always there.

Job 2:7-10 (KJV) "7) So went satan forth from the presence of the Lord, and smote Job with sore boils from the sole of his foot unto his crown. 8) And he took him a potsherd to scrape himself withal; and he sat down among the ashes. 9) Then said his wife unto him, Dost thou still retain thine integrity? Curse God, and die. 10) But he said unto her, Thou speakest as one of the foolish women speaketh. What? Shall we receive good at the hand of God and shall we not receive evil" In all this did not Job sin with his lips".

Pain often causes us to pray more and seek God's delivering power. However, for others it brings them to a point of giving up, not wanting to go on with life.

We tend to allow our emotions to cloud our judgment or our thinking, but Job in this last passage holds fast to his trust and faith in God.

We find again that Job is being attacked in his body with sores and boils all over his body and he scraped himself until the skin and scabs were falling off his body. But now enters his wife. Instead of being supportive or compassionate, she says to him, "will you still hold on to your integrity, curse God and die".

Maybe she just couldn't stand to see her husband going through so much. Maybe she was tired of seeing him crying or in so much pain.

Whatever the reason, Job could not give up on what he knew about God. It's a wonderful thing to know God in your heart. It's a wonderful thing to know for certain that no matter how difficult things may be, God's promises are real, and they will never fail you.

Advice from friends or loved ones can be such that it brings us into a state of confusion in our spiritual mind. We must remain confident in who we know God to be. God is our healer, he is our deliverer, our strong tower, and he is our way maker.

If God allows these problems or horrific situations to come our way, there must be a purpose for it. God creates strength within us by teaching us to overcome adversity.

Job didn't fall into the trap of blaming God, but he simply replied by saying, shall we reap the good in our lives and not the bad? Job wanted us as readers to realize that everyday won't be great. We're going to have good days and we're going to have some not so good days, but God is still good, and he is working on our behalf.

Job's example to us was not to sin by blaming God but to hold on to God's hand. Not give up.

The Apostle Paul echoed that sentiment in his statement to the church of Corinth in,

1 Corinthians 15:58 "Therefore my beloved brethren, be ye steadfast, unmoveable, always abounding in the work of the Lord, forasmuch as ye know that your labor is not in vain in the Lord".

Job's entire life was purposed for us to relate with him in dealing with all of life's difficult situations.

He illustrates how our reactions should be when trouble arises, when we receive bad news, when we receive bad advice from our friends or family, when we are feeling down and depressed.

After losing everything, Job suffered through his adversity, rebuked the enemy, and humbled himself before God again. God blessed him to have more than he ever had.

Job 42:10-13 (KJV) "10) And the Lord turned the captivity of Job, when he prayed for his friends; also the Lord gave Job

twice as much as he had before. 11) Then cam there unto him all his brethren, and all his sisters and all they that had been his acquaintance before, and did eat bread with him in his house: and they bemoaned him and comforted him over all the evil that the Lord had brought upon him: every man also gave him a piece of money and everyone an earing of gold. 12) So the Lord blessed the latter end of Job more than his beginning: for he had fourteen thousand sheep, and six thousand camels, and a thousand yoke of oxen, and a thousand she asses. 13) He had also seven sons and three daughters."

Haggai 2:9 (KJV) " The glory of this latter house shall be greater than of the former, saith the Lord of hosts; and in this place will I give peace, saith the Lord of hosts"

"And we know that all things work together for good to those who love God, to those who are the called according to his purpose". Romans 8:28

Hope is a feeling that too often gets lost in the middle of despair. Sometimes when there is no one to encourage you to keep getting up after being knocked down or to keep striving forward.

There are times when sickness, addiction, or financial struggles get you so depressed that it just seems as though there isn't hope for a better life. It begins to feel as though this state of living is normal.

Fridays after the mines closed, the drinking would begin. This occurred every weekend and as a young person, I thought this was normal. I didn't know any better because this was the impression I received of life.

But as I grew up, I encountered people who encouraged me to push myself and strive for excellence. They saw something in me that I couldn't see for myself.

As I got older, I found myself in a crisis. I became addicted to cocaine and felt as though I would never overcome such a horrible problem.

There was a day that I consumed so much of the drug that I collapsed on the bathroom floor, just laying there waiting to die. I had overdosed. I cried to the Lord and he picked me up and I began to feel better. However, addiction is strong and if you're not completely serious about being delivered, you never will.

While lying there waiting to die, the Lord spoke to me and asked whether I wanted to live or die. I cried with a voice of sincerity and desperation that I wanted to live.

The Lord delivered me from that addiction that night and I've never looked back

Often, we don't understand that God is working things out for us because it appears that nothing is happening. It looks as though we're stuck and all alone.

God is always there. When we can't see Him working, when we can't feel Him working, you must know that He is working things out on your behalf. It is God's desire that we live in a blessed stated of life. Again, we have purpose, our lives do matter and God's promise to always be there for us is real.

Deuteronomy 31:6 (KJV) "Be strong and of a good courage, fear not, nor be afraid of them; for the Lord, your God, he it is that doth go with thee; he will not fail you or forsake you".

Struggle will bring you more of the presence of God, if you can only realize that your life matters, not only to you, but family, friends, and even your enemies.

"But My God Shall Supply All Your Needs According To His Riches In Glory By Christ Jesus" Philippians 4:19

In our reading thus far, we have read about people's lives that didn't have any real high expectations out of life. However, God used them in wonderful and amazing ways to illustrate to us that we all matter and that we all have a purpose in life.

God can bring you from the lowest place in your life and place you in places you never thought you could go or achieve things you never thought possible.

Everyone matters and everyone is important to the kingdom of God. God's love for us is so strong that He will find you in your deepest mess and bring you through it without hurt or harm.

Our faith must remain strong, even when things seem to be their worst. Often when things are happening dramatically in our lives, we tend to let it consume us to a point where our judgment becomes clouded, and we end up making bad decisions.

We must understand that our problems or circumstances build our faith. If we didn't have them, we wouldn't draw close to God. We must not be defined by our problems or situations, but we must be defined by how we respond to life's issues.

There are moments in our life when our heartaches or

disappointments knock us down to our lowest points and often because they hurt so badly, we stay down in our sorrows.

As we stay down in our low places, we tend to get the agonizing feeling of being all alone or have the feelings of shame or guilt. Unable to pick ourselves up.

There was a man in the bible named Mephibosheth. His story can be found in 2 Samuel Chapter 9. Mephibosheth was the son of Jonathan and grandson of King Saul. After his father and grandfather were killed, his nurse fled with him, but he was injured and couldn't walk.

Due to his injury or his handicap, he became left out of things, he felt unworthy and that his life, no matter who is father or grandfather were, no longer mattered.

He resided in a town called Lo-debar. The bible describes this city as a lowly place. But what he didn't know was that the love of a King was about to bring him out of that place.

Isn't it wonderful to know that the love of our King, Jesus Christ, is searching us out, ready to bring us through our difficult times and rescue us from depths of our hardships?

God's love will find you no matter where you are. Whether you are lost and alone, displaced by tragedy, or in a lowly state of living. Don't be dismayed or be afraid or embarrassed. God's love is just a heartbeat away.

2 Samuel 9:1-10 (KJV) "1) And David said, is there yet any that is left of the house of Saul, that I may shew him kindness for Jonathan's sake? 2) And there was of the house of Saul a servant whose name was Ziba. And when they had called him unto David, the King said unto him, Art thou Ziba? And he said, thy servant is he. 3) And the King said, Is there not yet any of the house of Saul that I may shew the kindness of God unto him? And Ziba said unto the King, Jonathan hat yet a son, which is lame on his feet. 4) And the King said unto him, Where is he? And Ziba said unto the King, Behold he is in the house of Machir, the son of Ammiel, in Lo-debar. 5) Then King David sent, and fetched him out of the house of Machir, the son of Ammiel, from Lo-debar. 6) Now when Mephibosheth, the son of Jonathan, the son of Saul, was come unto David, he fell on his face and did reverence. And David said, Mephibosheth and he answered, Behold thy servant! 7) And David said unto him, fear not: for I will surely shew thee kindness for Jonathan thy father's sake, and will restore thee all the land of Saul thy father: and thou shall eat bread at my table continually. 8) And he bowed himself, and said, What is thy servant, that thou shouldest look upon such a dead dog as I am? 9) Then the King called to Ziba, Saul's servant, and said unto him, I have given unto thy master's son all that pertained to Saul and to all his house. 10) Thou therefore, and thy son's and thy servants, shall till the land for him, and thou shalt bring in the fruits, that thy masters son may have food to eat: but Mephibosheth thy masters son shall eat bread always at my table. Now Ziba had fifteen sons and twenty servants."

Mephibosheth probably felt as though no one cared for him, with no family, crippled, and with nothing to look forward to. But the love of a King was searching for him.

When Mephibosheth came before King David, he didn't know why he had been summoned, so his natural feeling was that of fear. Why would the King be looking for me?

Why would the King want me to come to his home? He felt unworthy to be in his presence.

He spoke to the King, feeling unworthy to be in midst of such a man. He even spoke of himself as being a "dead dog".

Mephibosheth was feeling low in his spirit, so much that he couldn't see that love was lifting him out of his circumstance. Reminds me of an old hymn "Love Lifted Me"

He had become so used to living in a depressive state that he couldn't imagine that anyone, especially the King, would care about him.

Some of us have grown up in communities where people didn't think much about us. I know I did. I grew up in McDowell County, West Virginia and during the mining days, it was a great place to live. There were lots of families with love for one another and respect for everyone.

As the mines closed, so did the clothing stores, then the mom and pop stores, and finally most small business. The People begin to move to other states to find jobs to take care of their families.

More and more people left and the county began to lose out on many things. There are still remnants of that time, however not much remains. People outside of McDowell County, West Virginia look upon the residents there as different. However, I was raised to have faith and trust in God. Believing that no matter my living situation, I'm still important and one day my King Jesus will call me to dine at his table forever. We all have purpose, and someone needs you. Someone needs to see how good God has been to you to believe that he will be just as kind to them.

Mephibosheth may have felt like his life had no meaning, but someone was seeking him out to bless him because of who he was. They are looking for you to bless you just because of who you are. You are strong, you are mighty, and you are victorious.

Sometimes we feel hopeless, unwanted, or even unneeded, but the truth of the matter is that someone is depending on you to remain positive, uplifted, and joyful. This brings about a change in someone who has been down and out, in need of a life changing experience.

David called Mephibosheth to him to give him a life changing opportunity. He had been handicapped most of his life, unable to do the things others were able to do. He was dependent on others to carry out the day to day things for him. He was a descendent of royalty, however not treated as such. But now the King was calling for him and he was restored land unto him, he was now given servants that once served his father and grandfather, and he now would eat at the Kings table forever.

His story is important because it epitomizes coming from nothing to now having everything.

As you go through this life, you must know that God is always there and is waiting for the opportunity to bless you with a new life. All you must do is listen for the call from the King.

God will do with you as he did with Mephibosheth and give you a life unimaginable. Let the love of the King, our Lord come to you and bring you from being underneath to being on top.

Your story is just as important as Mephibosheth's and your life has as much purpose as his and your life will turn around and be just as blessed. You're created by God and your life has meaning, it has purpose.

Be confident and trust that God didn't bring you all this way in your life to leave you now. Scripture promises that our latter, our future shall be greater than our past.

"The Lord Said Unto My Lord, Sit Thou At My Right Hand Until I Make Thine Enemies Thy Footstool" Psalms 110:1

At the beginning of this book we examined the young life of Joseph. His brothers were so jealous of him, that they sold him into slavery. They were thinking this would be the end of Joseph, and they wouldn't have to worry about him anymore.

However, we must understand that when God has a purpose for you, nothing nor no one can stop you from fulfilling that purpose.

Many people may have written you off, gave up on you, and threw you to the side like you don't matter. But what they don't understand is that you were predestined to greatness from the time you were in your mother's womb.

Jeremiah 1:5 (GW), "Before I formed you in the womb, I knew you. Before you were born, I set you apart for my holy purpose. I appointed you to be a prophet to the nations".

Joseph went through so much. He was enslaved, and then bought by Potiphar, the Captain of the Guard. But because it seemed that everything he touched prospered he was put over everything he had.

He oversaw the household and all his business affairs. Then Potiphar's wife lied on him and he was subsequently arrested and thrown into jail.

Then because God's favor was on his life so much, he

was thereafter put in control of the jail, and then released back to Potiphar.

Joseph went through all this trouble due to the actions of his family, his brothers. But what they didn't know was that Joseph was alive, and God had been blessing him mightily.

Joseph's life truly had purpose, and his story had to be told because we need to understand that God will do great things on our behalf if we just keep the faith. There is more to us than meets the eye.

I'm a believer that when people treat you wrong God will cause them to need you. He will cause your enemies to be your footstool. He uses the wrong they have done to you to be your step ladder to higher and greater things in life.

Joseph had interpreted a dream Pharaoh had which reflected a famine to come in the land of Egypt that would last for seven years.

Genesis 41:28-36 (KJV), "28) This is the thing which I have spoken to Pharaoh: What God is about to do, he sheweth unto Pharaoh. 29) Behold, there come seven years of great plenty throughout all the land of Egypt: 30) And there shall arise after them seven years of famine; and all the plenty shall be forgotten in the land of Egypt; and the famine shall consume the land; 31) And the plenty shall not be known in the land by reason of that famine following; for it shall be very grievous. 32) And for that dream was doubled unto Pharaoh twice; it is because the thing is established by God, and God will shortly bring it to pass. 33) Now therefore let Pharaoh look out a man discreet and wise and set him over the land of Egypt. 34) Let Pharaoh do this, and let him appoint officers over the Land and take up the fifth part of the Land of Egypt in the seven plenteous years. 35) And let them gather all the food of those good years that come and lay up corn under the hand of Pharaoh, and let them keep food in the cities. 36) And that food shall be for store to the land against the seven years of famine, which shall be in the land of Egypt; that the land perish not through the famine."

Joseph was born with a purpose. Never could he have imagined as a young child that he would suffer and prosper like he had. His life was up and down.

His life was changing daily. Opportunities were always presenting themselves to him and Pharaoh had such confidence and trust in him that he was about to appoint him as a ruler in the land and put over all of Egypt.

Often, we go through life's up's and down's not understanding the process that God was doing in your life in order to elevate you to higher positions.

Due to the mistreatment from the hands of his family, in particular his brothers, he was put in a position to achieve the great things God was doing and about to do in his life.

Genesis 41:38-43 (KJV), "38) And Pharaoh said unto his servants, Can we find such a one as this is a man in whom the Spirit of God is? 39) And Pharaoh said unto Joseph, Forasmuch as God hath shewed thee all this, there is none so discreet and wise as thou art: 40) Thou shalt be over my house, and according unto thy word shall all my people by ruled: only in the throne will I be greater than thou. 41) And Pharaoh said unto Joseph, See I have set thee over all the land of Egypt. 42) And Pharaoh took off his ring from his hand and put it upon Josephs hand, and arrayed him in vestures of fine linen

> and put a gold chain about his neck; 43) And he made him to ride in the second chariot which he had; and they cried before him, Bow the knee: and he made him ruler over all the land of Egypt."

Joseph, because of the things that had happened to him, because of all the hatred of his brother's, was now in a position to rule all of Egypt.

His life had taken a new and powerful direction. God often uses people's hatred or jealousy towards us as a way to reveal his power or favor within us.

Joseph's life didn't matter to his family, but it did matter to God. God loved Joseph so much that when he was being mistreated, God began to show just how much he truly cared for him and gave him the best of life.

Joseph's brothers had forgotten about him. After they sold him off to slavery they went about their way, doing whatever they wanted to with no regard as to what they had done to their brother.

My grandmother taught me to treat everyone with respect and love because you never know when you may need that person. Included in her message was that we should treat others as we would want to be treated.

> *Matthew 7:12 (KJV), "Therefore all things whatsoever ye would that men should do to you, do ye even so to them: for this is the law and the prophets".*

Joseph's brothers had so much resentment towards him that they couldn't love him much less respect him, but what they couldn't see was that God had Joseph's back and would always take care of him.

We will soon see what God does to those who treat his

people wrong. You must understand that God has a plan for you, and it will be perfected in you.

Jeremiah 29:11 (New International Version), "For I know the plans I have for you, declares the Lord, plans to prosper you and not to harm you, plans to give you hope and a future".

God recognizes the strength and abilities inside you and has determined from your birth the direction your life would go. He often allows the troubles of this world to come to you to make you a stronger, more powerful person.

This is exactly what was happening to Joseph. God's plan for him was manifesting itself very clearly.

I was taught as a child that we shall reap what we sow. Scripture reveals the truth of the phrase and although Joseph's brothers couldn't see the damage that they had done to themselves by the mistreatment of their brother, they were about to experience the consequences of their dirty deed.

Galations 6:7&8 (KJV), "7) Be not deceived; God is not mocked: for whatsoever a man soweth, that shall he also reap. 8) For he that soweth to his flesh shall of the flesh reap corruption; but he that soweth to the Spirit, shall of the Spirit reap life everlasting".

Previously Joseph had interpreted a dream that Pharaoh had which revealed that a famine would come upon the land, with seven years of plenty and then seven years of famine.

The dream instructed Pharaoh to begin to appoint someone to oversee the storage of food during the years of plenty to prepare for the famine. Joseph was chosen and excelled in the process, and Egypt would endure the famine due to his efforts.

The years of plenty were over, and the beginning of the famine has started.

> *Genesis 41:53-57 (KJV), "53) And the seven years of plenteousness that was in the Land of Egypt were ended. 54) And the seven years of dearth began to come, according as Joseph had said: and the dearth was in all lands; but in all the land of Egypt there was bread, 55) And when all the land of Egypt was famished, the people cried to Pharaoh for bread: and Pharaoh said unto all the Egyptians, Go unto Joseph; what he saith to you, do. 56) And the famine was over all the face of the earth. And Joseph opened all the storehouses, and sold unto the Egyptians; and the famine waxed sore in the land of Egypt. 57) And all countries came into Egypt to Joseph for to buy corn: because that all famine was so sore in all lands."*

We see the famine had started and quickly spread throughout Egypt and all countries. Joseph, by the leading of God, had begun to store up food enough that Egypt could survive.

However, people from outside the city experienced the severe effects of the famine and could not find food.

Again, we must reverence how important it is to treat one another with love and respect. Opportunity may present itself, in that the very one you mistreat will be the very one you need.

Isn't it something that people can mistreat you, with no regard of your life or feelings and when trouble comes to them, they don't hesitate to come crying to you for help?

I find it disturbing that people would have the nerve to ask someone for help after they have treated others so harshly, as Joseph's brothers had done to him.

But as we have read, Joseph is no ordinary person. He was a person whom God predestined with purpose. He was born to be that true example of when the enemy tries to destroy your life, God will not only bring you out of that circumstance, but elevate your status, double your finances, or place you in positions of authority.

As the famine has spread, it has now reached the land of Joseph's family and they are suffering.

Genesis 42: 1-2 (KJV), "1) Now when Jacob saw that there was corn in Egypt, Jacob said unto his sons why do ye look one upon another? 2) And he said, Behold, I have heard that there is corn in Egypt: get you down thither, and buy for us thence; that we may live and not die."

Now that Joseph was Governor in Egypt the people had to come to him to purchase food. Now his brothers had come to Egypt to purchase food but had no idea that the one they had to purchase food from would be the brother they tried to destroy.

Joseph had been through so much and undoubtedly missed his family but probably couldn't be more thankful for how his life had turned out.

Sometimes when we endure difficult hardships we tend to give up and not see how God is molding our lives. He shows us that no matter the condition our lives appear to be in, we are important to the advancing of his people and his kingdom.

We need to look past our situations and speak positively

over our lives. You have purpose and you matter.

Now the brothers came to purchase food and bowed themselves before the Governor. Looking upon them, Joseph recognized them but they didn't recognize him.

Why was it that they couldn't recognize Joseph? Well, Joseph was a young teenager when he was sold into slavery and now almost 20 years had passed since that time.

His brothers never expected to see him again. They assumed him to be dead. His father may have thought and cried for him with memories, but his brothers never gave another thought. In fact, they probably couldn't recognize him because they had done all they could to forget him. They would never dream they would see him again.

Genesis 42:6-8 (KJV), "6) And Joseph was the governor over the land, and he it was that sold to all the people of the land: and Joseph's Brethren came, and bowed down themselves before him with their faces to the earth. 7) And Joseph saw his brethren and he knew them, but made himself strange unto them, and spoke roughly unto them; and he said unto them, Whence come ye? And they said, From the land of Canaan to buy food. 8) And Joseph knew his brethren but they knew him not."

Upon seeing his brothers, it would be safe to say that many emotions ran through Josephs mind.

He probably felt confused, not knowing exactly what to do or say. He probably was angry, and then he was probably happy to see them since he hadn't seen them since he was a young teenager.

But one thing became increasingly clear as in verse number 7, that he spoke roughly to them.

Joseph could have treated them harshly, but he remembered the dreams he had of them when he was a young teenager, and he could not mistreat them.

He accused them of being spies and put them in jail. But after three days, he let them go.

He gave them corn to take back to their families and gave all their money back. Due to this his brothers began to have guilty feelings and questioned themselves as to why he was treating them with such respect.

Joseph kept one brother and commanded the others to return home with their corn and when they returned to Egypt to bring back their youngest brother. Now they were afraid because of what they had done to Joseph years before.

My belief is that we live a life of decisions and consequences. We may just be reaping the consequences of decisions we have made earlier in life. I often tell my children and grandchildren that every decision will come back to them either in a good way or a bad way, but it will come back to them.

This appears true to Joseph's brothers that they were feeling guilty due to the decision they had made to cause harm to Joseph.

Even though they tried to forget about the unjust act they committed against Joseph, it was apparent that they had not.

One could say that they probably had these guilty feelings every time something went wrong in their lives. Every time a disheartening situation came upon them or every time someone mistreated them, they probably condemned themselves and credited these things to the egregious act they committed on Joseph.

No one should expect to do wrong to someone and get away with it without consequence. Every action demands a reaction. Every decision we make comes back to us either in a good way or a bad, but it does come back full circle, and this is what the brothers were finding out.

Genesis 42:21-22 (KJV), "21) And they said one to another, We are verily guilty concerning our brother, in that we saw the anguish of his soul when he besought us, and we would not hear; therefore is this distress come upon us. 22) And Reuben answered them, saying, Spake I unto you, saying, Do not sin against the child: and ye would not hear? Therefore, behold, also his blood is required."

This scripture also reminds me of another scripture about doing harm to God's people.

1 Chronicles 16:22 (KJV), "Saying, Touch not mine anointed, and do my prophets no harm".

This should be encouragement to us all, to know that our lives matter so much to God, that when others come up against us to cause us harm, God will not allow them to prosper.

God will not allow anyone to prosper or rise in social status when they knock you down in their attempt to get there.

As the famine spread in the land, it was so bad that Joseph's family once again found themselves without food and their families were suffering. Their father directed them to return to Egypt to purchase more corn.

Now a confrontation was set to happen to reveal Josephs

identity to his brothers. All that had happened in his life, although physically caused by the actions of his brothers, was orchestrated by the hand of the Lord.

Joseph truly had purpose and had been used by God to be in place to save his family.

I pose this question to you. Are you able to forgive someone who continually mistreats or despitefully uses you? Can you forgive someone who purposely causes undo hardship in your life?

Joseph realized that God had blessed him many times over. Every time the enemy tried him, God blessed him more.

Genesis 45:1-8 (KJV), "1) Then Joseph could not refrain himself before all them that stood by him: and he cried, Cause every man to go out from me. And there stood no man with him, while Joseph made himself known unto his brethren. 2) And he wept aloud: and the Egyptians and the house of Pharaoh heard. 3) And Joseph said unto his brethren, I am Joseph; doth my father yet live? And his brethren could not answer him; for they were troubled at his presence. 4) And Joseph said unto his brethren, Come near to me, I pray you. And they came near. And he said, I am Joseph your brother, whom ye sold into Egypt. 5) Now therefore be not grieved, nor angry with yourselves, that ye sold me hither: for God did send me before you to preserve life, 6) For these two years hath the famine been in the land: and yet there are five years, in which there shall neither be earing nor harvest. 7) And God sent me before you to preserve you a posterity in the earth, and to save your lives by a great deliverance. 8) So now it was not you that sent me hither, but God: and he hath made me father to

Pharaoh and the lord of all his house, and a ruler throughout all the land of Egypt."

Joseph still loved his brothers and provides to us a Godly example of a God-fearing man by forgiving his brothers for what they had done to him. He further explains this had to be done because it wasn't them, but God that caused this in order to provide for them and save their lives.

This is a perfect illustration of how we should look at turmoil in our lives. There is a reason and a purpose behind all that happens in our lives.

When we look back at earlier scripture regarding the dream that Joseph told his family, we can now see that God was showing Joseph his future. His dream revealed that his family would become submissive to him, and this was brought to his remembrance.

We can see that everything within the dream, the sheaves, sun, moon, and eleven stars were representative of his parents and his eleven (11) brothers.

God sees who you are and no matter what comes your way, the purpose he has instilled within you will come forth. You must remain faithful and prayerful. God will take care of you and allow you to receive the best life has for you.

Going further, as Joseph is crying loudly due to being reunited with his family, Pharaoh has heard what is happening and seeks to bless the family all because of Joseph. Wow! Look how God is blessing everyone associated with Joseph. Amazing!

Pharaoh instructs Joseph to tell his brothers to go back home, get their father and all their household and come back to reside in Egypt. He advised them not to worry about bringing their stuff for all of Egypt was theirs.

Joseph's brothers, their households, and their father, Jacob, began their journey back to Egypt as directed by Pharaoh through Joseph.

When they arrived in the land of Goshen, Joseph met them and hugged his father's neck for a long time, for this was the first time he had seen him since he was a teenager. Can you imagine the emotions he must have felt, seeing his father for the first time since his early teens?

His father undoubtedly had the same emotions, remembering the love he had for his young son before he was sold into slavery by his brothers.

Joseph told his family that he would go before Pharaoh and present them to him so that he may bless them and cause them to have land and employment.

It's such an amazing turn-around! To see a young Joseph, who was put down by his brothers, hated by his brothers, and eventually sold into slavery by his brothers, now found himself needed by his brothers.

This also shows the heart of a man who knew the real meaning of love. People who have been wronged by others often seek revenge in many ways.

Joseph could have had his revenge against his family but instead decided to turn the other cheek and show the Godliness within him.

This was probably because God had blessed Joseph so much throughout his entire ordeal. Every time it looked as though it may be the end for him, God blessed him not only to overcome, but to prosper. A thought now comes to mind, "you may be down, but you're not counted out".

Joseph had realized that his life had purpose and now his family needed him after all they had done to him.

Joseph could have resented them and had his revenge on them, but he chose the Godly approach by allowing the Spirit of Christ inside of him to direct his actions instead of his flesh.

> *Genesis 46:29-34 (KJV), "29) And Joseph made ready his chariot, and went up to meet Israel, his father, to Goshen, and presented himself unto him; and he fell on his neck, and wept on his neck a good while. 30) And Israel said unto Joseph, Now let me die since I have seen thy face, because thou art yet alive. 31) And Joseph said unto his brethren, and unto his father's house, I will go up and shew Pharaoh, and say unto him, My brethren, and my father's house, which were in the land of Canaan, are come unto me; 32) And the men are shepherds, for their trade hath been to feed cattle; and they have brought their flocks, and their herds, and all that they have. 33) And it shall come to pass, when Pharaoh shall call you, and shall say, What is your occupation? 34) That ye shall say, Thy servants' trade hath been about cattle from our youth even until now, both we, and also our fathers; that ye may dwell in the land of Goshen; for every shepherd is an abomination unto the Egyptians".*

Joseph endured the harshness of all the effects that come with jealousy and hatred; and became a man of authority who would eventually be the man his brothers would come running to for help. Isn't this ironic?

Many us you been mistreated over time by those who didn't or couldn't see how special you are and/or the plans

God would have for you.

How have you treated those people? Have you sought revenge against them, or have you allowed the Spirit of Christ lead you to forgiveness?

Forgiveness empowers you. It's often viewed as being weak and giving power to them who have done you wrong. However, this is not the truth. Forgiveness empowers you and shows the strength of God in your life. When you're able to find forgiveness in your heart for those who have wronged you it reveals to the world that you are growing in strength and obedience in the Word of God.

Joseph not only forgave his brothers but explained that all they had done had put him in position to save their lives. This love was important, as it allowed Joseph to place them in position to have a bright future.

Genesis 47:1-6 (KJV), "1) Then Joseph came and told Pharaoh and said, My father and my brethren and their flocks, and their herds, and all that they have are come out of the land of Canaan; and behold, they are in the land of Goshen. 2) And he took some of his brethren, even five men, and presented them unto Pharaoh. 3) And Pharaoh said unto his brethren, what is your occupation? And they said unto Pharaoh, Thy servants' are shepherds, both we, and also our fathers. 4) They said moreover unto Pharaoh, For to sojourn in the land are we come; for thy servants have no pasture for their flocks; for the famine is sore in the land of Canaan: Now therefore, we pray thee, let thy servants dwell in the land of Goshen. 5) And Pharaoh spake unto Joseph, saying, Thy father and thy brethren are come unto thee: 6) The land of Egypt is before thee; in the best of the land make thy father and brethren to dwell; in the land of Goshen let them dwell: and if thou knowest any men of activity among them, then make them rulers over my cattle".

The thought that drove me to write this book was to show everyone just how special they are and that their lives matters. So much tragedy around us, so much homelessness, so much hatred, causes us to have a poor mindset which lead to decreased hope.

When we look at our communities, cities, and states, we see the harsh effects that life had on so many. Many of our youth and young adults are committing suicide due to a lack of hope.

So many people are living with the belief that they don't matter, that no one cares about them, and that they don't have purpose.

You may not realize how important you are, how much your life matters to others and the Kingdom of God.

Life often kicks us while we are down, making it so hard to get up and have the faith to believe we can go on to achieve greater things in this life.

Suffering, health conditions, loneliness, and financial difficulties can cause us to have a negative state of mind, and if not careful, we can fall into a state of depression. You are important and the enemy knows that God has use of you, and therefore causes so many situations to arise in your life to keep you battling until you lose hope.

I pray that you have found encouragement in the reading of this book and have seen the examples of those whose lives were full of despair, but God brought them out of their problems and blessed them beyond measure.

God blessed Joseph and brought him out of the pit into the palace. He was placed over everything Egypt had to offer, all of this as a slave.

God blessed the woman with the issue of blood that she endured for twelve long years. Determined to be unlearned and dirty, however, God cleaned her up and healed her body after she stretched out on her faith.

God blessed Job after losing his fortune, his children, and servants. Job kept his faith and love for God, even after his wife wanted him to give up on God and die, even after his friends were trying to get him to admit that he must have sinned to have caused all the hurt in his life. However, God brought him out of his suffering and doubled his life's possessions.

God blessed Mephibosheth, bringing him out of lo-debar, where he was handicapped and living in conditions not pleasing to him. King David was searching for someone of the lineage of Saul to bless and now Mephibosheth was blessed with servants and would eat at the table of the King for as long as he lived.

All of these people had a purpose for living. Their stories are relative to us today as we see that God can change horrible situations into blessings.

I pray that you have been encouraged and have seen the true examples of those whose lives were full of despair, but God brought them out of all their problems and blessed them beyond measure.

Their lives, their stories are important to us because they are wonderful examples of how our faith should remain strong, no matter how detrimental life appears.

Remember you are fearfully and wonderfully made and when the enemy attacks your life it's because he knows that your life is important and has purpose.

As you go on with your everyday life, whether you are having a good day or a bad day, remember the stories and examples provided in this book and say within yourself, If God did it for them, He surely can do it for me, because my life matters.

May God bless you, may God keep you, and may God's glory forever surround your life.

To God Be the Glory.

TESTIMONIALS

Pastor Lockett, I would first like to say "Thank You" for affording me such an opportunity! It has been a privilege and an honor to read, "Your Life Matters." This could not have come at a more pressing time in my life. As I struggled with depression, uncertainty, fear, and loneliness- you provided the outlet that helped me weather the storm. You reminded me, "Without a test, you have no testimony!" You managed to illustrate the power we possess as believers and the endurance of our Faith.

You have given us life's tool kit for a better you. You even touched on dealing with those who persecute us. As humans, we have to remind ourselves that the battle is not ours, it's the Lord's.

Pastor Lockett, you have gifted us with the perfect guide to everyday life and the trials that follow. May God continue to bless you! You are a true inspiration to us all.
Tamika, Northfork, WV

Elder Lockett's book, "Your Life Matters" is a book of encouragement to all those who find themselves struggling with the daily issues of life. It gives biblical focus on how God can and will turn things around for us, if we trust him. Sometimes we go through the storm and rain, but we can make it if we stay focused. One of my favorite quotes from this book is, "Don't allow your past to determine your future". This lets us know that we must first forgive ourselves, realize our life matters, and then move forward.

This book is exciting, beautifully written, it's factual with supporting scriptures, and it will help us all remember, yes, our life does matter. If this book gives hope to one person, then Elder Lockett's effort in writing will not have been in vain. You are invited to read, enjoy and tell someone who is going through, "Yes, our lives really matter!!!"

Pastor Donna E. Jackson, Crumpler, WV

This book really hit home for me, and it really touched my heart. Sometimes when going through trials and tribulations and when I feel like nothing is going right for me, I come to realize that I am a child of the King and that my life matters and has purpose. If find myself examining my life and I seem to get frustrated because I feel I should be further along in life that I am, so jealousy, low self-esteem, anger, doubt, and fear start flowing inside of me.

I know that is not God's plan and also that is not what he wants me to feel so I start encouraging myself by singing songs, praying for guidance, that he will lead me in the right direction and into his will, to stay positive, start moving forward, pressing on to conquer and fulfill the desires that God has for me.

At the end of the day I know that I am a strong, beautiful, smart, Godly woman, and my life does truly matter. Thank you, Pastor Lockett for writing this book it is

a real encouragement to me and I know it will be to others as well. Thank you, Jesus.
  Sonya D, Pulaski, VA

"Your life Matters" is a wonderful and powerful tool that can and will bring encouragement to those who feel like all hope is gone. Life's trials and tribulations are often difficult and bring us to a hopeless state of life. But God is our hope and our strength and this book reveals that your life is very important and you truly have purpose. Thank you, Pastor Lockett for giving us such an incredible tool to help us through our difficult times.
  Tonya L., Princeton, WV

www.ingramcontent.com/pod-product-compliance
Lightning Source LLC
Chambersburg PA
CBHW070438010526
44118CB00014B/2094